STEPPING INTO SCIENCE

THINGS TO DO WITH WATER

By Illa Podendorf

Illustrations by Larry Winborg

CHILDRENS PRESS, CHICAGO

Illa Podendorf, former Chairman of the Science Department of the Laboratory Schools, University of Chicago, has prepared this series of books with emphasis on the processes of science. The content is selected from the main branches of science — biology, physics, and chemistry — but the thrust is on the process skills which are essential in scientific work. Some of the processes emphasized are observing, classifying, communicating, measuring, inferring, and predicting. The treatment is intellectually stimulating which makes it occupy an active part in a child's thinking. This is important in all general education of children.

  This book, THINGS TO DO WITH WATER, provides opportunities for experience in making predictions. These predictions are based upon data previously observed and recorded.

Copyright © 1971 by Regensteiner Publishing Enterprises, Inc.
All rights reserved. Published simultaneously in Canada.
Printed in the United States of America

Library of Congress Catalog Card Number: 78-148583

CONTENTS

Water in Many Shapes 4
Water in Many Colors 11
Water, Here and There 19
Water in Many Measures 26
Water, Many Temperatures 41
Things to Do 48

WATER IN MANY SHAPES

Susan spilled some water on her desk.

"Look," she said. "The water is shaped like a doll."

Dan had to agree. The spot was shaped a little like a doll.

Susan poured a little water on a tray. This time the water was shaped more like little balls.

Dan said, "Water is a liquid. It has no shape of its own."

Dan poured water into a glass
that was square on each side.

He poured water into a rectangular-shaped glass.

Then he poured some into a bowl.

It was easy to see the shape the water was in each of these things.

Can you decide what shape the water is in each of these glasses?

Can you tell which is shaped like a cylinder, and which is shaped like a cone?

Susan and Dan put water into these things. They put them in the freezer.
 Can you predict what shapes the water will be when it turns to ice?

Were your predictions good ones? The pieces of ice are solid. When the ice shapes melt, what shape will the water be? Water is a liquid.

WATER IN MANY COLORS

Susan dropped one drop of clear red coloring into a glass of clear water. She watched the coloring move down into the water. One drop of red coloring did not make the water very red.

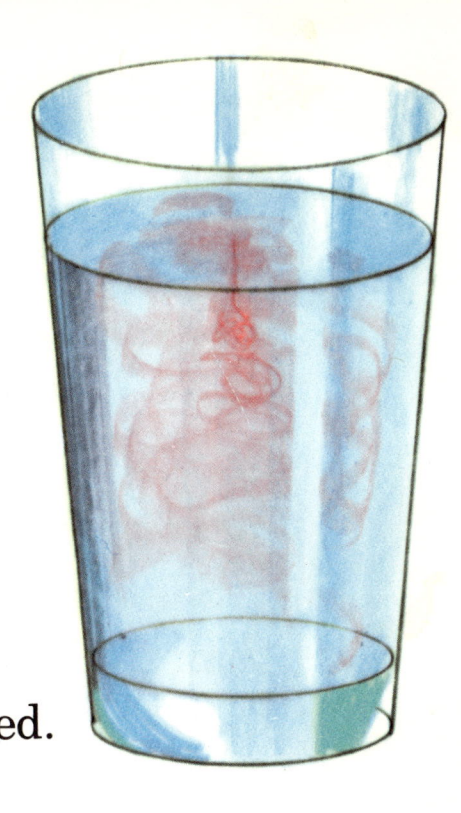

She put twelve drops of red coloring into a glass of clear water. The water became very red this time.

Susan predicted what would happen when she put *three* drops of red coloring into a glass of clear water.

She said, "It will be more red than the first one, and less red than the second one."

Was her prediction a good one?

She could not have made such a prediction if she had not first tried *one* drop, and then *twelve* drops.

She could only have made a *guess*.

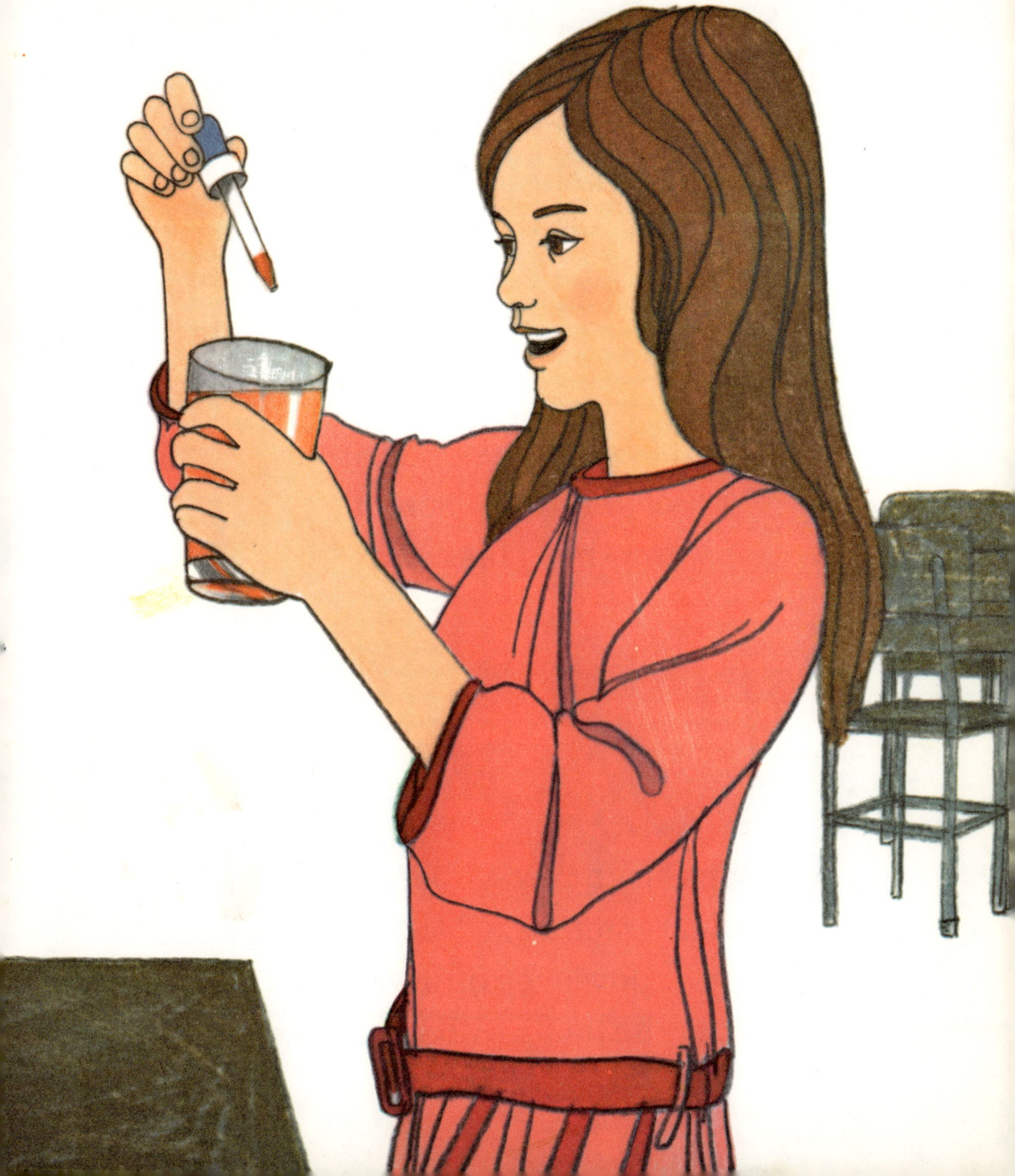

Susan dropped four drops of blue coloring into a glass of clear water. She thought this made a nice shade of blue.

She added four drops of yellow coloring to another glass of water.

Then Susan remembered something. Susan remembered that when she colored yellow over blue with her crayons, she had a different color.

She predicted that if she mixed half of the blue water with half of the yellow water she would have green.

This is the blue and yellow water mixed.

Do you think Susan's prediction was a good one?

You might use your blue and yellow crayons and make a picture that has green in it.

Susan made some more predictions.

She predicted what color she would have if she mixed blue water with red water.

She predicted the color she would have if she mixed yellow water with red water.

Crayons will help you make your own predictions.

The next page will show you what Susan predicted.

Is this what you predicted, too?

WATER, HERE AND THERE

Susan put a spoonful of water in each of two small, flat dishes. She covered one of them, and set both of them in the window.

See what happened.

The water in the dish that was not covered had disappeared into the air.

This time Susan put two spoonfuls of water in each of two other dishes.

She thought the one without the cover would become empty first.

Do you think this was a good prediction? It was.

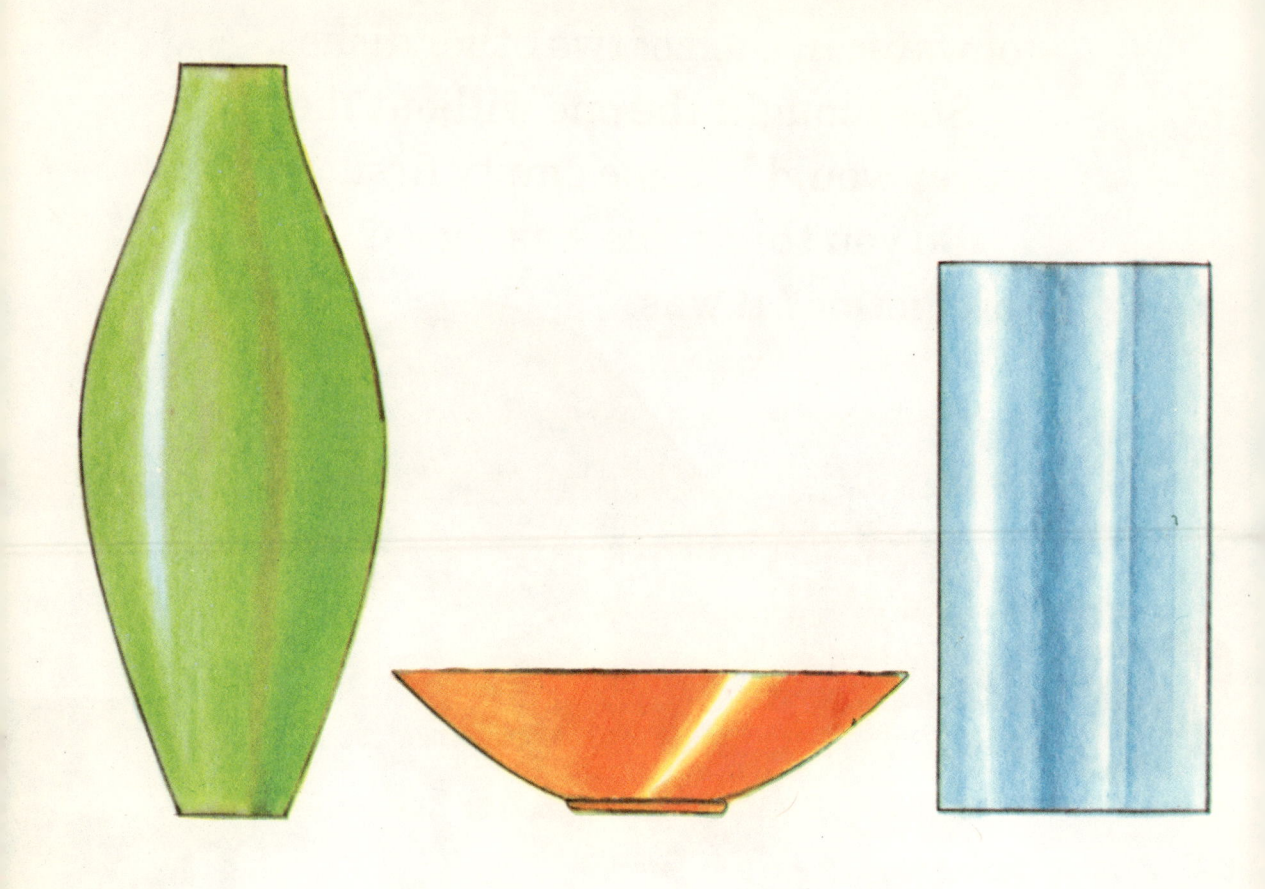

Susan found three dishes with different shapes. She put a spoonful of water in each of them and set them in the window.

She predicted that the water in the flat dish would disappear first, and that the water in the tallest one would disappear last.

   Why do you think Susan made that prediction? Perhaps she thought that the tallest dish was the most like the covered dish.

   It was a good prediction.

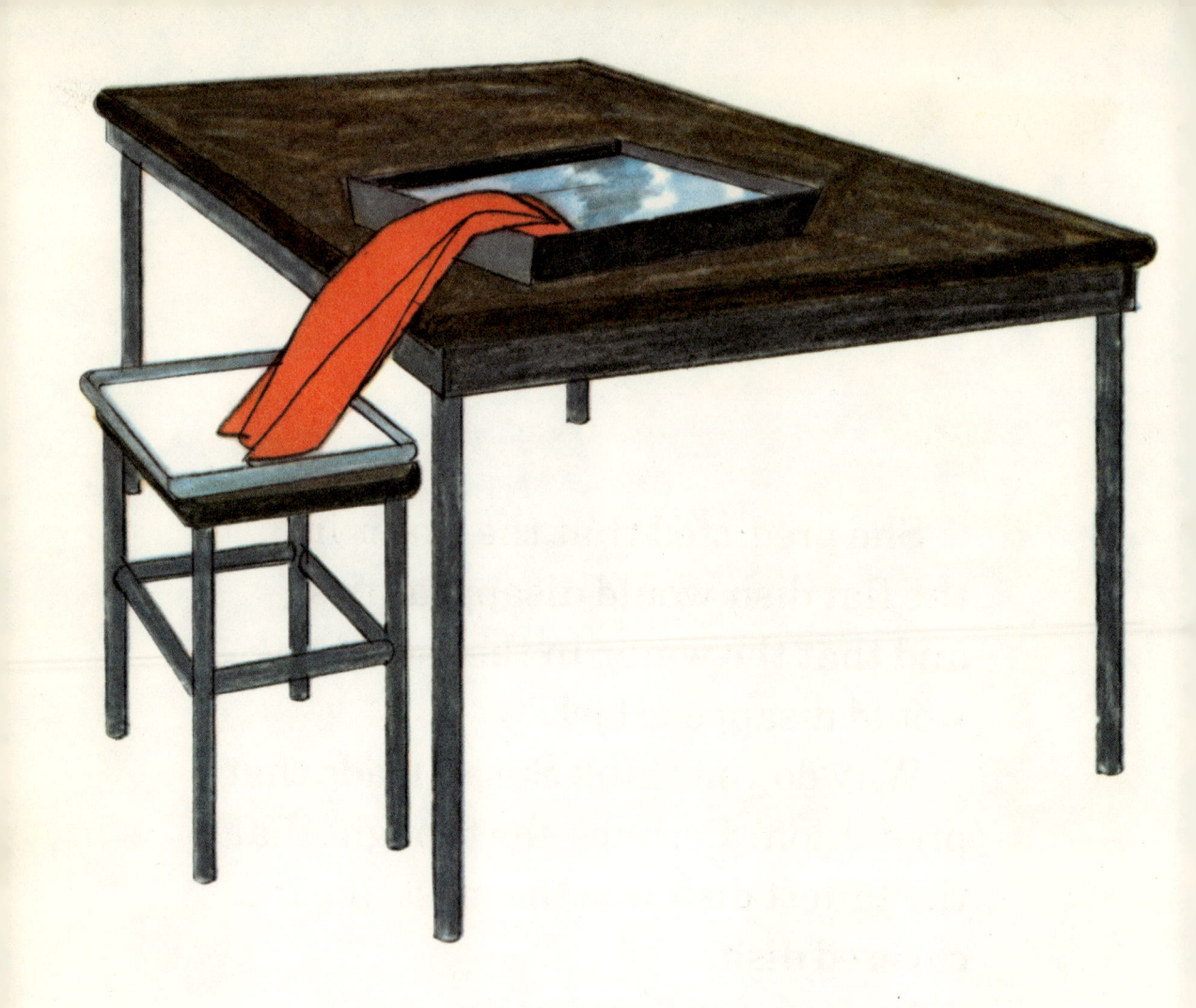

Susan took a long piece of dry towel. She put one end of it in a pan of water. The other end hung down on a tray.

She predicted that the towel would become wet all over.

Something more happened.
What was it?

WATER IN MANY MEASURES

Susan tried to find out how
many drops her dropper would hold.
First she counted twelve drops.

Then she counted
ten drops,

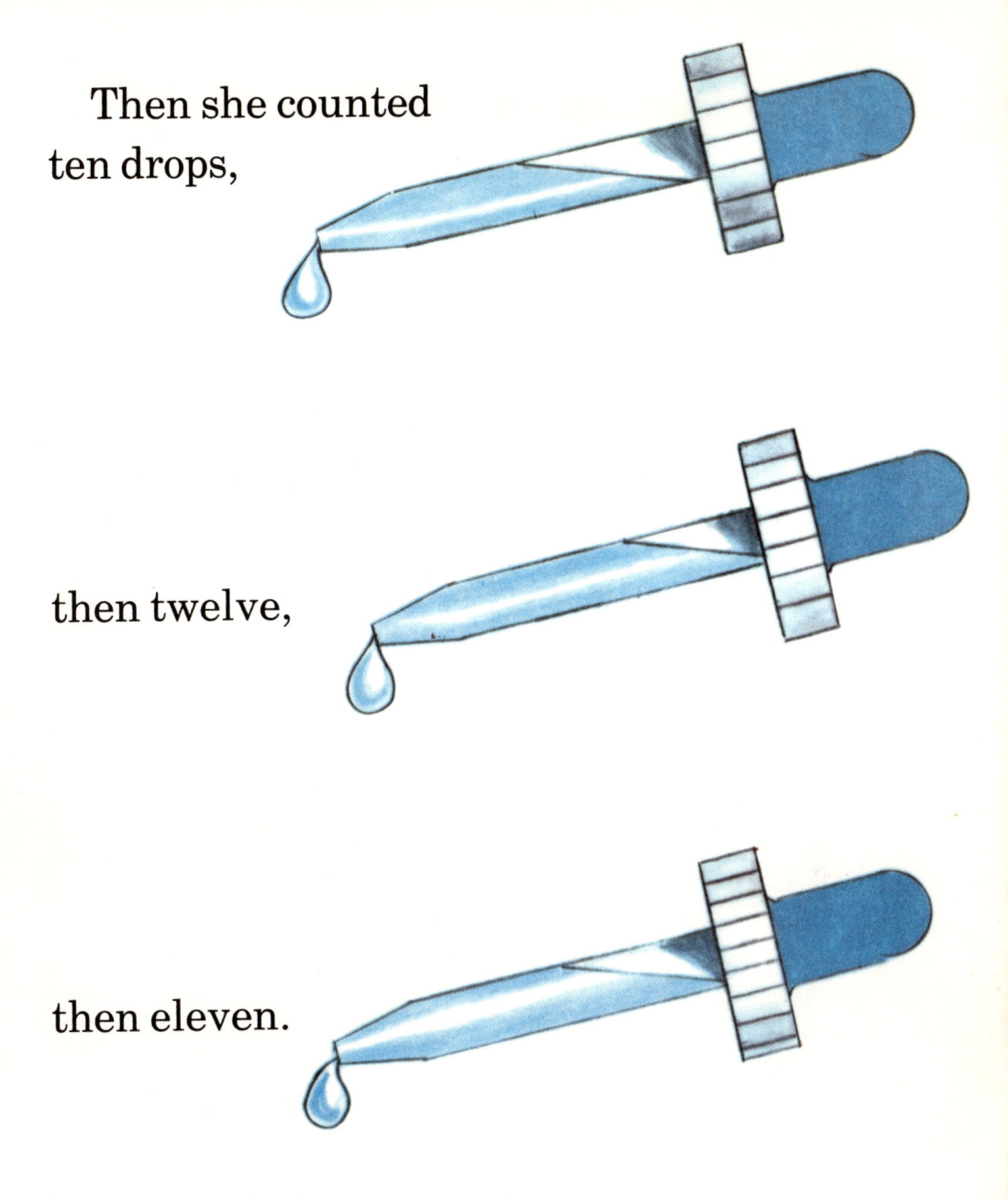

then twelve,

then eleven.

She decided that twelve was
about right.

Dan had a dropper, too.
It looked a little bigger than Susan's. She counted fifteen drops each time she used it.

Susan's mother had a much bigger dropper.

Susan predicted that it held at least forty drops.

Dan predicted that it held many more drops than that.

They based their predictions on what happened when they tried the other two droppers.

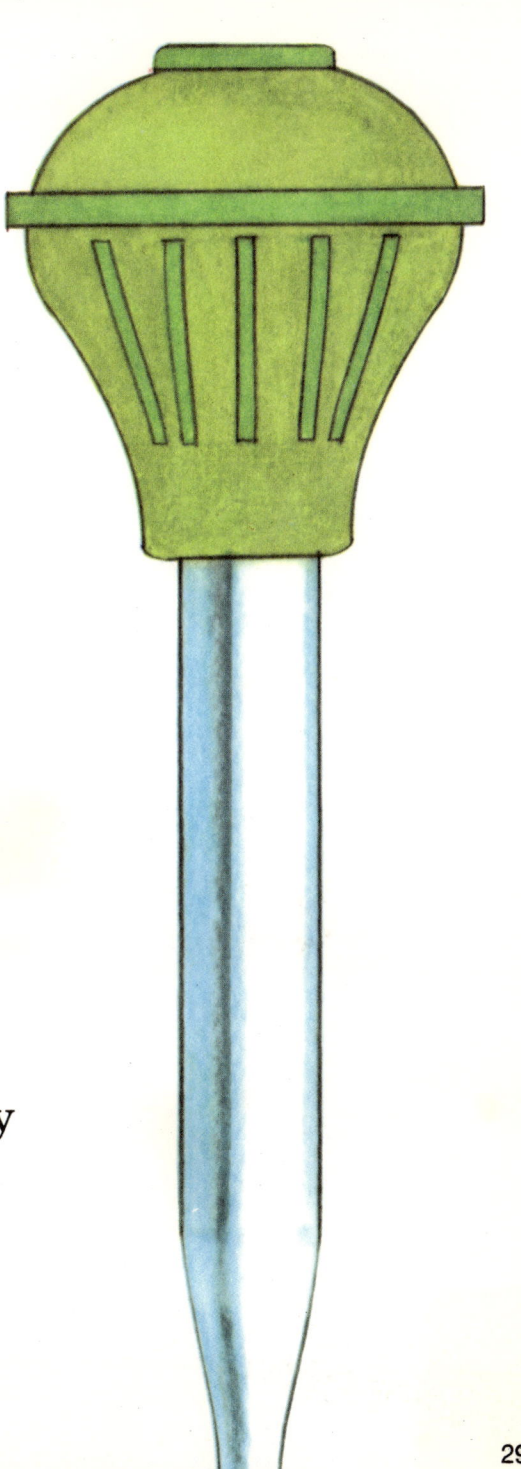

Susan tried to test the big dropper. But the water ran out so fast that she could not count the drops.

She knew that the big dropper held more drops than the smaller ones. But she did not know how many, because she could not count them.

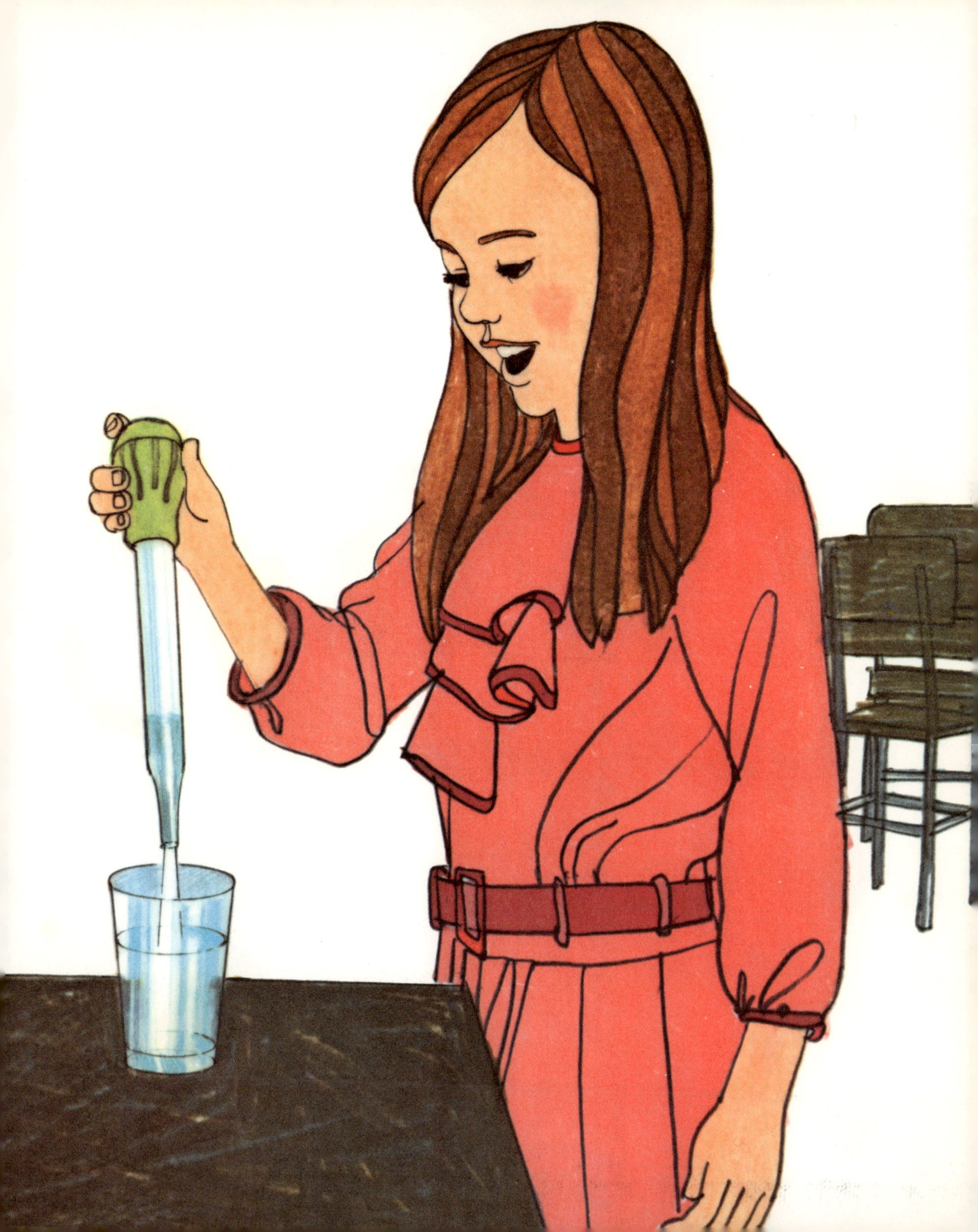

Counting drops is only one way to measure a liquid.

Perhaps Susan should have used one of these units of measure.

Dan had a tall glass jar, about half-full of water.

He made a mark at the top of the water in the jar.

He also had several lead sinkers, all the same size.

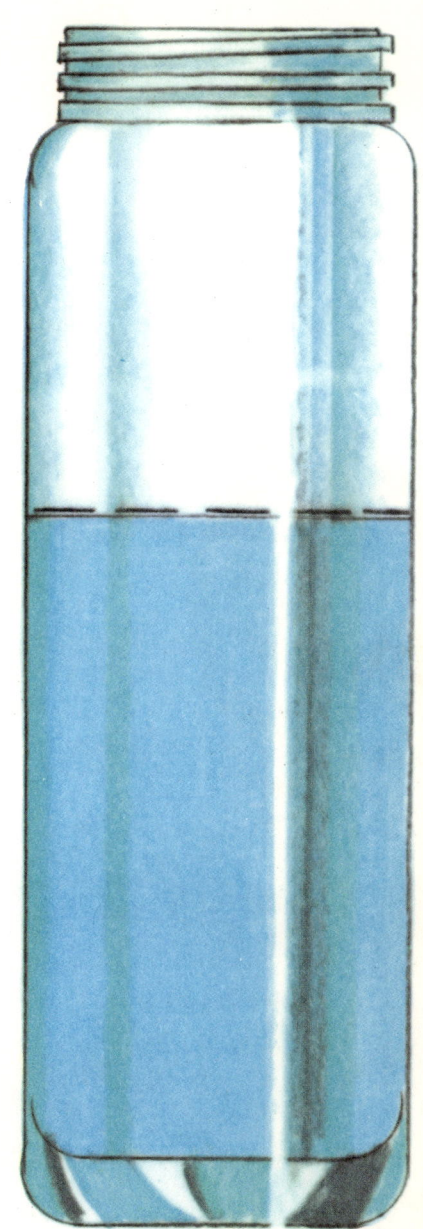

Dan lowered one sinker into the jar.
He marked the top of the water.

He lowered
a second sinker,
and made a third
mark.
He lowered
a third sinker,
and made another
mark.

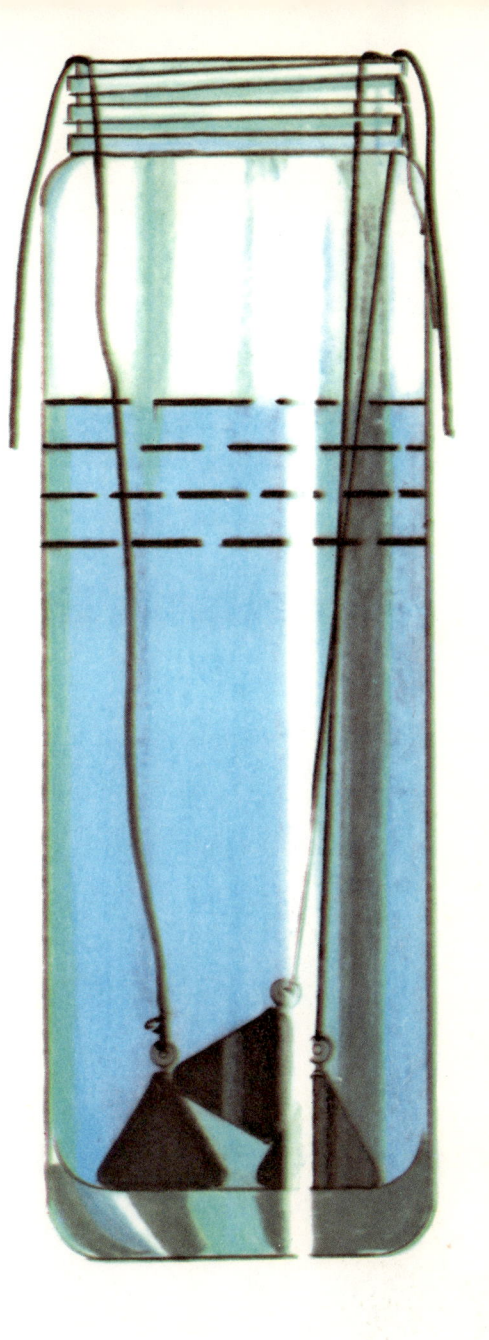

Each sinker made the water rise
to another height.

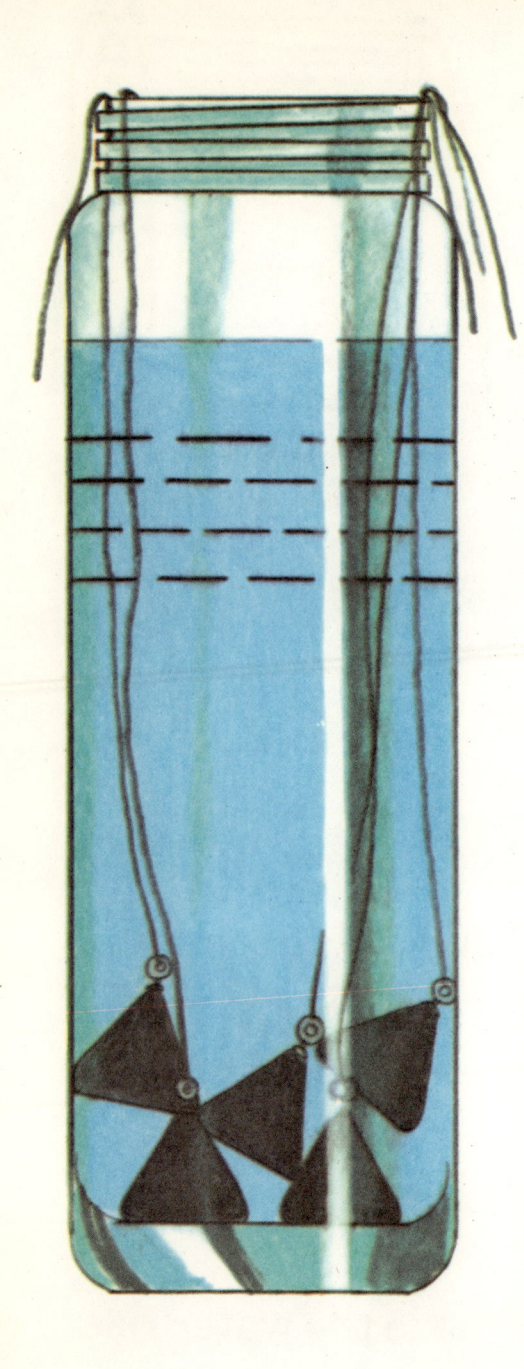

Then Dan decided to put in two more sinkers at once.

See where the water is now.

Where do you think it would have been if he had put in just one more instead of two?

Dan showed Susan how to make a graph of the water and the sinkers.

Can you see where the mark would have been, if he had put in only one sinker instead of two? There would have been four sinkers instead of five.

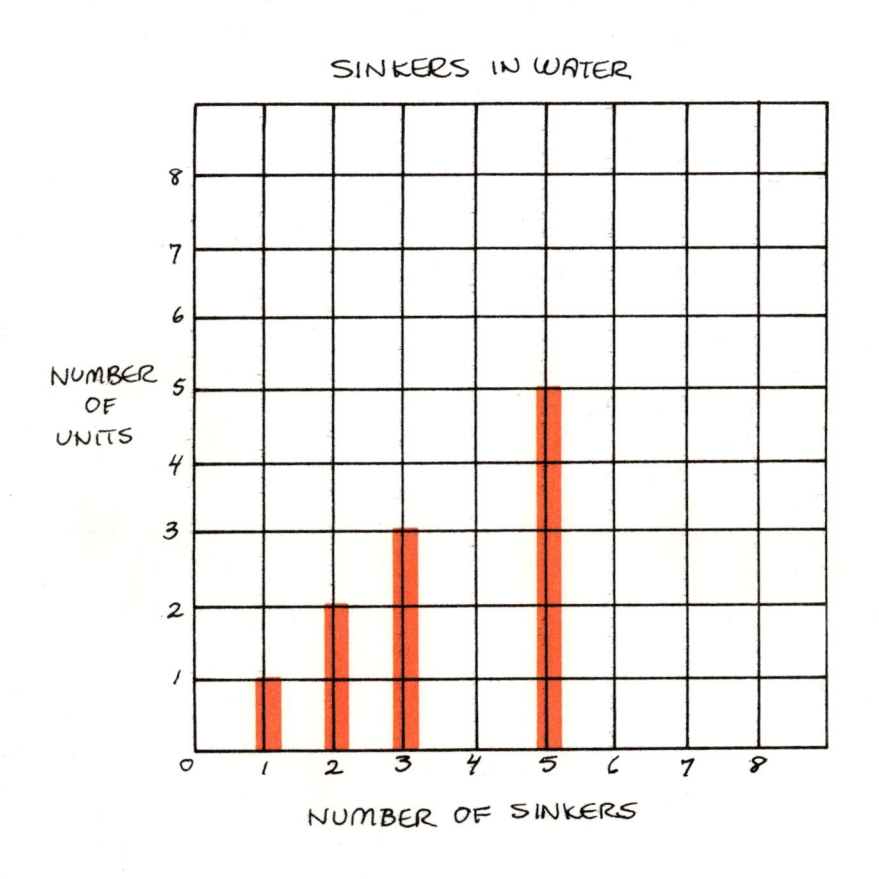

Susan predicted that the graph would have looked like this with four sinkers in the water.

It is easy to make predictions when you have a graph.

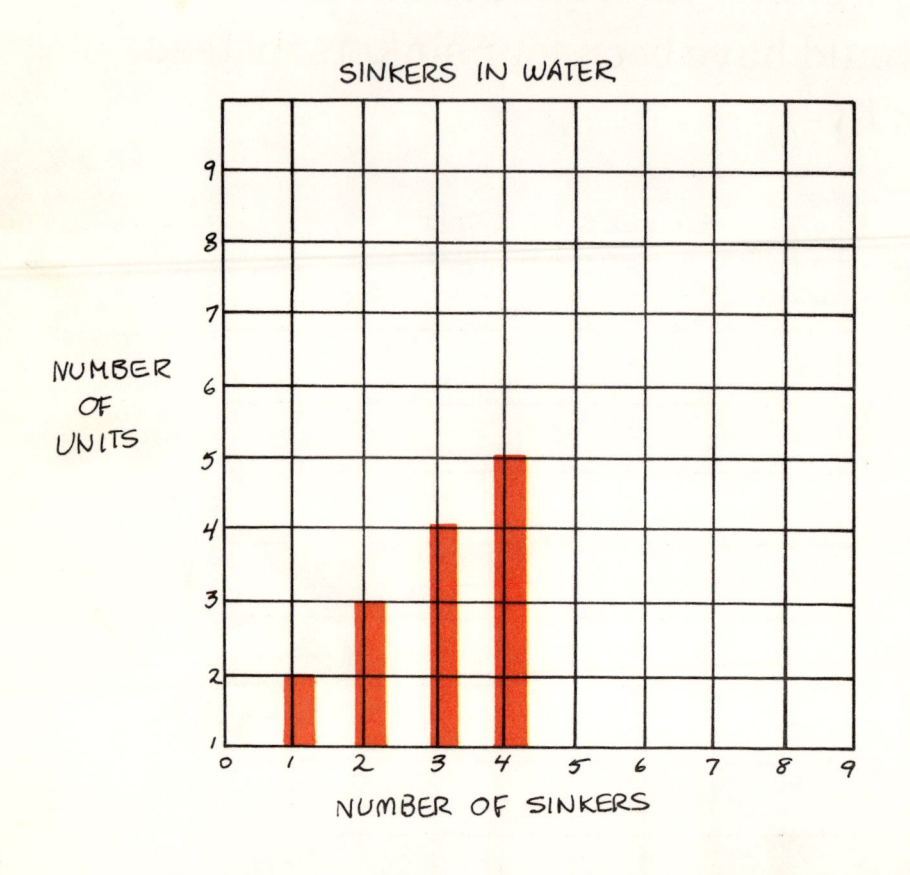

SINKERS IN WATER

NUMBER OF UNITS

NUMBER OF SINKERS

Dan pulled out one sinker to see if her prediction was right. It was.

SINKERS IN WATER

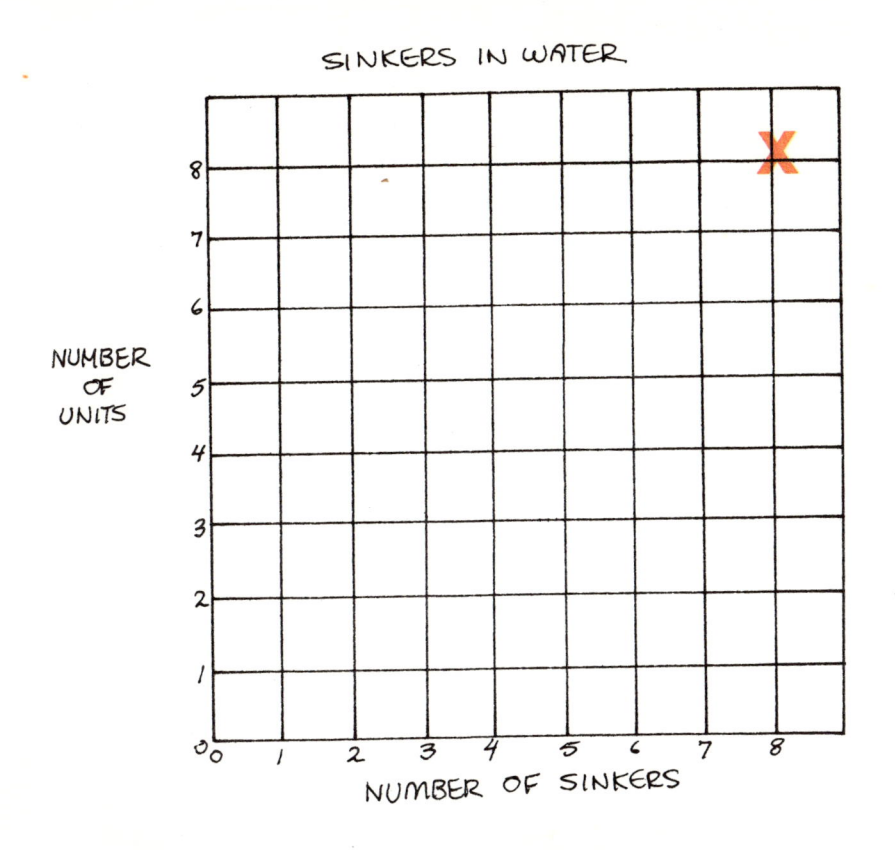

NUMBER OF UNITS

NUMBER OF SINKERS

Susan predicted that if she put eight sinkers in the water, it would be eight units high. She marked the graph to show her prediction.

SINKERS IN WATER

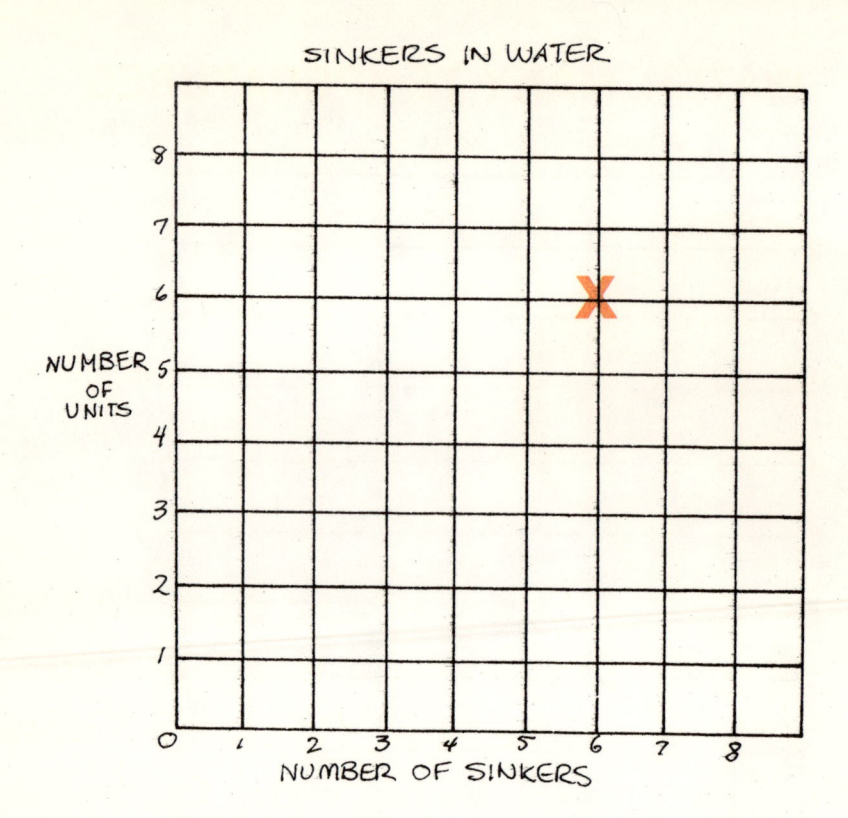

(graph: NUMBER OF UNITS vs NUMBER OF SINKERS, with an X marked at (6, 6))

Susan predicted that if she pulled out two sinkers, and left only six, the water would be six units high.

Do you agree with Susan's prediction?

Can you make other predictions?

Perhaps you can find a jar and sinkers and test them.

WATER, MANY TEMPERATURES

Susan filled a glass with water from the cold-water faucet.

She filled a glass with water from the hot-water faucet.

Susan felt the water in both glasses. She could tell that one was warmer than the other, but she could only guess what the temperatures were.

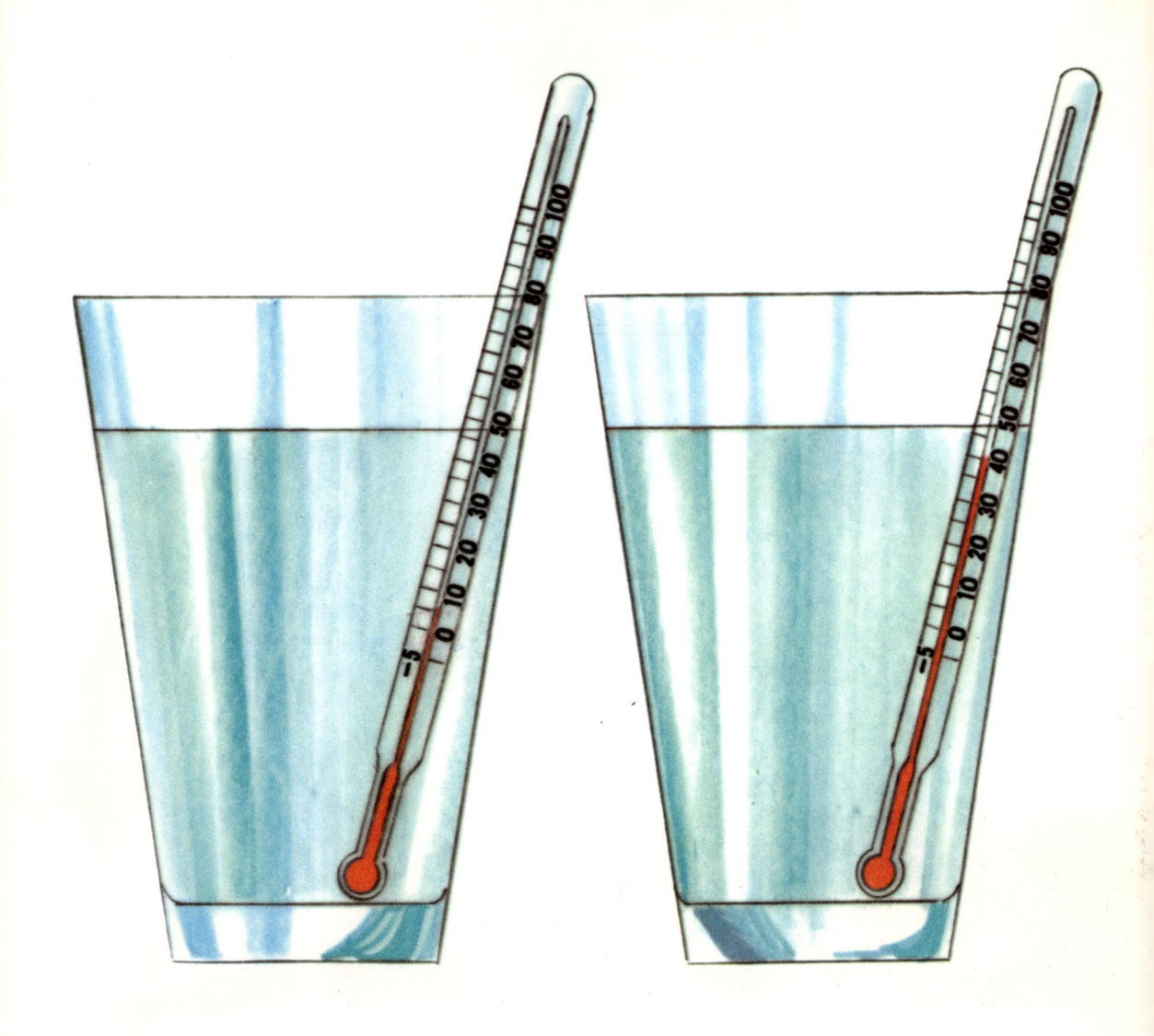

Susan put a Celsius thermometer in each glass of water. Now she could see what the temperatures were.

Susan poured about half of the cold water into a third glass. Then she poured in half of the hot water.

She knew what the temperatures of each had been. Now she could make a prediction.

She predicted that the water in the third glass would have a temperature of about 25 degrees Celsius.

She used a thermometer to test her prediction. Was it a good one?

Susan put a thermometer in another glass of water. The temperature of the water was 30 degrees Celsius.

She put two ice cubes in the water and predicted that it would be colder. You are sure to agree with this prediction.

This is what she found out.

The temperature after one minute.

The temperature after two minutes.

You might try this, too. The temperatures you get may be different because of the size of the glass and the ice cubes. But you can predict safely that the water will get colder and colder until the ice is gone.

THINGS TO DO

Pour water into a strange-shaped vase. What shape is the water?

How many colors can you make with red, yellow, and blue water?

How many different units of measure can you find?

Can you predict temperatures of water? Do your predictions improve with practice?

You can make predictions if you base them on things you know.